I DESERVE A RAISE

...SO HOW DO I CONVINCE MY BOSS?

Career management
recommendations and skills for people
to increase their **value to an**
employer!

STACIE GARLIEB

TABLE OF CONTENTS

Introduction v

My skills and experience are more valuable than my co-workers I think ... 1

I go above and beyond more often than anyone else at work I think ... 3

I look for ways to help my co-workers with their job I think ... 5

I use my leadership skills in formal and informal ways I think ... 9

I'm an expert at lots of things that make me valuable in my job I think ... 13

I ask how I can make my boss' job easier for him I think ... 15

My volunteering outside of work should count for something I think ... 17

I know how to write the measured parts of my performance review I think ... 23

I understand how to write the subjective parts of my performance review I think ... 27

I communicate my expectations for professional development to my boss I think ... 33

Introduction

Everyone would love to make six or seven figures as a base salary – the more zeros the better. Companies have changed the ways they evaluate each job and the value it provides to the organization due to industry and competitive shifts. Employees need to think outside the box too and take ownership of their professional progress. Thinking that you deserve more money is very different than showing you deserve more money. Depending on your job function, you may believe that since you do your job well, meet all the expectations, and get along with your co-workers, so of course you should get a pay increase.

This may or may not be true. Even if you have received an increase in prior years, next year the company may need to make changes in personnel, business strategy, or objectives due to reasons beyond your control. Smart employees don't wait for industry, company, or economic changes to suddenly be valuable to their employers. Use this book as an idea generator, personal motivator, or professional organizer to position yourself for not only your next pay increase, but every performance discussion you have throughout your career.

My skills and experience are more valuable than my co-workers **I think** ...

This is the 'what have you done for me lately' assessment for employees. Sure, when you were hired it was because you had more skills or experience than the other candidates. Depending on your tenure in the job, you may have proven to your boss that you were the best catch they ever hired. Maybe you are still in the 'proving phase' but are setting yourself up as an early leader in the team. Perhaps you have been in the job for a long time (at least in your mind) and know that you have mastered the basics.

The real evaluator of your skills and experience is your direct supervisor. But, who else on your team could influence your boss' impression of you and the skills you have? Think about who you interact with on a daily or weekly basis – co-workers, customers, other managers, direct reports, etc. What do they think about your skills and experience?

Some companies have integrated multiple opinions on an employee's skills and work through a process called 360 degree feedback. If you aren't familiar with this, it is a questionnaire that is confidentially sent to various people within the organization to solicit feedback on your performance. The data is tabulated in a cumulative format and then presented to you by HR or your manager. Each person can also provide comments that are blinded.

If your company is using this type of process, you will have a strategic decision to make – who should I send the questionnaires to? Some organizations will only let you pick one or two 'optional' respondents and then they force out the forms to anyone they know you interact with on a regular basis. Other companies are using the process to see who you are going to select and let you pick all of the people. Either way, who you pick is an important decision because this information goes into your HR file for eternity.

Employees who are limited to only a couple of people should select individuals who can verify your abilities to do your job function, but also to problem solve and do more. Those that can pick the entire group should spread the selection between different levels of your internal organization and any external organizations if possible. Don't just choose your buddies who you hang out with socially or at company meetings. That will be very obvious to your boss when the answers all come back like you walk on water.

Even if your company hasn't gotten to this point, it's important to realize that any point one of your co-workers could be asked about your work and how you support the team. This goes both ways. Taking an opportunity to recognize one of your teammates for their skills to your boss is a great way to show you are really looking for chances to make the whole group better. Your skills and experience may be greater than your co-workers, but the best way to show that to your boss is to not only consistently perform your own job, but also look for opportunities to support the team.

I go above and beyond more often than anyone else at work I think ...

When was the last time you read your job description or the list of general responsibilities in your role? Do you know exactly what basic job functions you need to perform to contribute your skills to the organization? People who can't easily answer 'what do you do?' at a social function will have a tough time justifying to the boss how they go above and beyond in that job. Sure, you can always consider your list of basic responsibilities and your job title and use that as your bar of measurement on whether you are doing more than anyone else. But is that really going to get you recognition from management or a pay increase?

The first step in really evaluating your actions and value in going above and beyond is to determine whether you should have a comparison to your colleagues. The criteria should be fact based and focused on the things you did, steps you took, and results you achieved. If you are involving a comparison to your colleagues at all, there needs to be a reason. For example, if you are a salesperson and there is a contest to get more feedback from customers on a service evaluation form, and you visited 15% more customers weekly to fill out the form by explaining the ultimate value to them in improving what the company provides them, that makes sense. By using that method, let's say you generated more forms than your peers, and therefore more feedback for the company to use to improve service. In this case, the comparison makes sense and does show how your efforts to go above and beyond make a difference.

This topic can be particularly volatile when employees describe their participation and skills on team projects. Be careful not to overstate your actual value versus your perceived value. Characterizing yourself as the 'team leader' could be ok even if you don't have that formal designation, as long as you have the details on what you did in that role to back it up. Think about what you specifically did that put you into that role and how the team, and ultimately the organization, benefited from you taking on that additional responsibility.

For those of you who don't want the leadership role, or prefer to do your job well but stay out of the spotlight, you may also be going above and beyond. In fact, you may be doing more that your peers, but it's possible that your desire to fly under the radar may be hurting your chances to get that next pay increase. Without standing up and yelling 'Hey, I just did something extra that you need to notice Mr. Manager!' you can identify your efforts to contribute beyond your basic role. Consider sending your supervisor an email outlining what and how you did the activity or project. Using a phrase at the end of the message such as 'As a result, we were able to X and I believe this will help the overall Y of our department'. Explaining your actions and understanding how that supports the organization will truly show your boss how you went above and beyond.

I look for ways to help my co-workers with their job I think ...

Scenario 1: Just last week, Tom the Co-Worker arrived at your desk and asked to borrow a pen. Being the team player that you are, you gave him one of your favorite pens and offered a pencil also. Scenario 2: Today, Sue the Co-Worker called you and shared her concern about finishing a project by the deadline at 5pm without having a report from another department. You know Jim in that department and offered to call him to expedite the report, which she greatly appreciated. She was able to complete her report and meet the deadline.

It may be obvious that Scenario 1 is not a big deal and really not noteworthy, while Scenario 2 definitely is a good example of making a positive impact by looking for a way to help your co-workers. The difference between the two is great in this case, but the principle is the same in terms of evaluation. Looking for ways to help, versus having a quick way to help fall in your lap. This isn't to say that ac-cidentally finding yourself in a position to provide assistance doesn't count. Remember in Chapter 1 that the perception your co-workers have of you could play a significant role in your performance evaluation or how your boss perceives you as a member of the team. Taking advantage of those spontaneous opportunities to assist are important too.

Looking for opportunities to help co-workers involves more active participation in your work environment. Again, those of you who want to 'fly under the radar' may not want to go here, but you run the risk of not being top of mind when the pay increases are handed out. Depending on your job function, you may not interact with a lot of people, so you may actually need to actually be strategic in how you approach contributing in this way. The easy options are to take advantage of situations when you can solve an existing problem or issue. Anytime you have a co-worker who shows up to a meeting or to your area of the workplace with statements like 'We have a problem' (obvious), or 'This is not going to work...' that's your cue to put on your thinking cap and determine how you can assist.

This doesn't mean you immediately go into Daddy/Mommy mode and start giving directions on how they should or could make the situation easier or solve the problem. Helping your co-workers in these situations is most effective when asking questions to support them in finding a viable way to get their job done, or to offer your skills to make the situation better. You don't want to put yourself into a position of being perceived as the department life raft on anyone's Titanic. Asking questions and offering suggestions forces your co-worker to think through issues and hopefully they are learning how to solve problems on their own in the future. Any boss will want their employees to be able to have greater critical thinking skills, so you are helping the whole team in the process.

Another opportunity will be when you identify – unsolicited – how to help others. Yes, it's the Golden Rule. Believe it or not, your boss will appreciate you looking for ways to help your team overall, and sometimes that means looking for ways to help certain people.

Here's an example – let's assume you are the most organized human on the planet when it comes to internal reporting. If the monthly report needs to be filed on the 1st, you have it to the boss by the 25th of the previous month. Bill the Co-Worker isn't really focused on organizational skills or administrative work. He wants to be out in the field talking with the customers or working on things that have an external impact. But, if the team doesn't all do their part of the administrative work, your boss is going to get an angry phone call from his boss.

In this case, you can't do Bill's reports for him – you could, but no one is actually benefiting in the end, and your boss (or the next one Bill has) will be stuck hounding him to get his reports in. You could have a private conversation with Bill and let him know how you are able to be so organized and get your reports in early.

But what is the motivation for Bill to change the way he is doing his reports? Maybe it's the fact that the boss recognizes you in meetings and tells other managers how you are the most organized person he has. Maybe it's the fact that you have more time to spend with family and friends because you aren't stressed about emails and voice mails at the end of the month asking you for the reports. Whatever keeps you motivated to send the reports in a timely fashion may not be the trigger that will work to motivate Bill, so be sensitive to what would be relevant to his motivation and needs. Thinking about your audience before you initiate the conversation is an important consideration before you address any issues or opportunities for development with peers that could assist your boss or the team overall.

The bottom line is that you don't have to be the 'Company Fireman' to look for ways to help your co-workers. The team players who are there as a resource for everyone and are viewed as an expert (keep reading for the chapter on this) are valuable. The leaders who try to be proactive in identifying the next issue or obstacle are valuable. The employees who will work behind the scenes to support team members with their strengths are valuable. Know thyself – whatever bucket(s) you fall into, keep your eyes and ears open to provide the most value to your organization overall.

I use my leadership skills in formal and informal ways I think ...

Leadership is a concept that some people do not want to embrace. Sports oriented people tend to be more comfortable identifying themselves and others as leaders. Depending on your involvement in school and extracurricular activities you may not want that label in the workplace. If you are preparing to ask for a pay increase, leadership is a word you need to understand and be able to identify as your role in different work experiences.

There are different types of leadership skills. Some of us were never the Team Captain or the President of the club in high school – that doesn't mean you weren't or aren't a leader. It also doesn't mean that if you haven't expressed your abilities in that type of role that you can't. The next chapter is going to identify the ways that someone may want to mentor or help others in a training function and that is definitely a way to show you are a leader. But there are other ways that you may want to consider exhibiting leadership depending on your position within an organization and how you want to add value to the company.

Think back to when you had a job in a restaurant or retail shop as a salesperson or server/host. Were you a leader? What happened when there was a customer who didn't like the meal or shirt that they purchased – did you call the manager over immediately and tell the customer 'it's not my fault, I don't make the pasta or clothes'. Probably not. First off, you talked to the customer and apologized for their inconvenience and told them that you wanted to make sure they were happy with your company. You may have had to bring management into the picture at some point, but you waited until you had the facts first.

Your current workplace should be treated in the same way. The best approach to using leadership in the workplace is not to think that you have to be in charge to be a leader. No one has to identify you as the person who makes the decisions or solves the problems – you can put yourself in that position on your own. Taking ownership of your role and handling obstacles makes you an informal leader.

Evaluating what skills and experience you can offer the team and then looking for ways to offer those is one of the most impactful professional steps you will take throughout your career. Sitting around waiting for someone to say 'you are really good at X' is not going to help your career path or the organization. Be honest about what the team needs and how you can provide it. Don't get too analytical about this – maybe there isn't a current need, so keep an open mind. Listen to people in meetings and team projects. If someone is telling you 'You are really good at X', 'I wish I could do Y', or 'That is something we all should be able to do' – jump on the chance to assist, coach, or train.

Those who are the on the 'leader' track internally need to be strategic also. There may be a manager who will be threatened by your attempt to show your skills. Even in a formal leadership position it is important to identify your audience and appropriately communicate and interact with them. This doesn't mean you need to back off and take a submissive position. It does mean that you should evaluate the political landscape for your organization and team. Think and act like a smart leader. Be selective about how you lead actively and passively to get the most favorable reception from people at all levels of the organization.

Some of us were the defined leaders early in our careers – the hot shots, superstars, ones to beat, first to be promoted… For the Gen X'ers and Baby Boomers who don't want to own those labels anymore and are happy to pass those roles to the Millenials, there is a process to make that transition work for the organization. First, you need to realize that your manager may not want someone else to take the role. You have been reliable in the role and they know your skills. Second, someone less tenured may not want to take on the role.

Passing the torch is a process – deciding to do it overnight will not help your career or that of your co-worker. Remember in the last chapter how you can help a co-worker? This is a significant way that you could support peers and assist your manager to have a legacy of skills that keep the team productive and developing no matter what stage you are at in your career.

It really doesn't matter what type of leader you are in the workplace. What matters is your honest evaluation of how you use your skills as a formal or informal leader to help your boss and the organization. Taking the time to identify how you are currently adding value as a leader and how you could potentially add value will give you areas to develop and discuss with your manager.

I'm an expert at lots of things that make me valuable in my job I think ...

No one goes into a job thinking that they are not going to be an 'expert' in some area over time. Yes, there are those people who are constantly humble, (refer to the 'fly under the radar' sections) and they may actually have the most flexibility and opportunity in the long term. For the employees who feel like certain areas of their skills could be defined as 'expert' by their employers or the industry, critically identifying those areas is important.

There are two crucial criteria in this category: Who identified you as an expert? and How can you share your expertise with others in the company? For employees who believe they are an expert because a co-worker or boss said so, there is another step for you to take. When did this happen, what was the circumstance, and most importantly, what have you done to continue to be an expert?

This may seem silly – once an expert, always an expert, right? It depends on the people who evaluate the expertise, and those who can benefit from the expertise. If you are an expert because a previous employer told you so, and you come into a new organization and don't actively use those skills, are you really an expert? Depending on the company, being an expert includes sharing that experience or skills with others in a mentoring or training capacity. If you don't want to do that, will that company value you as an expert?

For those who want to leverage their expertise, there are some considerations of how to express and manage these skills. First, establish a plan on how you achieved the skills and how you could share those with others on your team or in your company. If you received internal or external training to get the expertise, it is ok to share that resource with your peers.

Remember that the best way to identify your expertise is to communicate your interest and ability to share those skills within the organization. Maybe you can go through a traditional and formal process like the training department. Your boss may want you to share the information and skills with new hires or people who are not excelling in that area. If your organization is less formal or smaller, you may find that you are most effective in covertly helping your peers by talking with them 'offline'. Knowing which communication method will be the most effective in helping the organization will be important.

Tenure may have given you the confidence to consider yourself an expert. Being an expert doesn't mean that you can't or won't challenge yourself to improve your skills or keep up to date on the latest information for your job or industry. Finding new training or experi-ences that you can share to make you, or your internal or external customers, more revenue or more productive makes you a more valuable employee. For example, you may choose to sit back and ignore the value of using an iPad in your job, but if that is the direction your company or industry goes, you need to be the person who is ready to help others.

Sharing expertise is a talent that some people use throughout their entire career. Others want to keep their expertise to themselves. Overall those who are willing to help others will benefit on multiple levels. Your peers and management will recognize your efforts and you may end up with opportunities you wouldn't have had otherwise. In later chapters we will address how this can be a benefit to your professional growth in the short and long term.

I ask how I can make my boss'
job easier for him I think ...

Why do I need to make my boss' job easier? It really doesn't matter if you want to help your boss out of some philanthropic gesture or pure logic. Performance reviews, promotion discussions, and everything in between are built on your manager's evaluation of your ability to make their job easier and make the team better. Depending on your industry and job function it may be through management of other people, taking on projects, or owning certain responsibilities. Whatever it is – making your manager appreciate you is a necessary skill for your professional development.

Making your boss' job easier doesn't necessarily mean that you do part of his job for him. There are several ways you can help, including using your leadership skills as discussed in the previous chapter. If you have a manager who leads by consensus or loves the concept of 'team input', your leadership can help him. When he asks for recommendations on processes or ideas don't wait until everyone else comes up with an answer – jump in. By starting the conversation, you will motivate your peers to chime in and take the pressure off your boss to make the decision on his own.

The other obvious move is to actually ask your boss directly how you can help him. Be sensitive to your company's environment to pick your time to do this. Employees in highly competitive fields (i.e. sales) may consider you openly asking 'How can I help you?' in a meeting as 'brown nosing'. It could be part of your performance discussion, or some other less formal, one on one interaction. Keep your ears open for opportunities to ask him the question during the work week. If he is making comments about being overwhelmed with work or having a tight deadline, ask if there is something you can do to assist.

Don't forget the more subtle ways you can make your boss' job easier. Does his manager ask for best practices and feedback on company procedures, policies, or systems? If you have input that could be constructive, share that with your manager. Is your team struggling with some type of change in the company? Instead of contributing to group complaint sessions, listen and then offer an idea of how to approach the change in a positive way. Supporting your boss by contributing to positive communication and morale can be very impactful and greatly appreciated.

Depending on your relationship with your boss, you may also be able to assist them by sharing your expertise. As discussed in the previous chapter, helping a co-worker with a skill you excel at adds value to the team. There may be areas you are stronger at (organization, technical skills, etc.) than your boss too. Offering to help your boss continue his professional development in different areas will improve the team and company too.

My volunteering outside of work should
count for something I think ...

Work-life balance began as a catch phrase in the 80's to help managers talk to their employees about spending time outside of work instead of committing 80 hours a week to the job. Working moms were also popping up in every industry at the time, so their need to ulfill roles at home and the ofice created a new perspective on how managers should support their employees. Whether you volunteer to assist your community or for personal enjoyment, the balance you are adding to yourself as an employee could be valued in the workplace.

Volunteering comes in all shapes and sizes. Some types will be relevant in discussions with your peers and management at work and other types may be personal and not pertinent to any improvement in your career. The best way to evaluate whether your volunteering outside of work could count toward your overall career development is to identify what responsibilities and roles you have at the place(s) you volunteer and where the volunteering takes place.

If you are using skills in volunteering that are relevant on the job too – such as communication, organization, leadership etc. – you should consider making your manager aware of what you are doing. This is especially relevant for those of you who take on leadership roles in your volunteer work. Offering your skills to support others in this type of experience shows your employer that you are very committed to the results an organization achieves. Not many people want to sign up to assist a group with activities that they think could possibly be supporting a venture doomed to fail.

Being a leader outside of the workplace will also tell your manager that you are capable of that responsibility or activity at work. This is especially important if you haven't had a leadership role at work in the past and you want to pursue that type of responsibility in the future. Be careful not to fill your manager in on your personal activities if you don't want him to recommend you use those skills on the job too, though!

Another important consideration is where you volunteer and whether you want your manager to know about it. Obviously, if there could potentially be a controversial position (political, religious, etc.) the organization's objectives are focused at or a direct conflict with your place of work, keeping your involvement private would be a better strategy. Remember that your social media is another place to keep any details of your participation in private mode if that is the decision you make. Ultimately, you should evaluate the risk to benefit ratio of sharing information with your peers and co-workers about what you are actively involved in after hours or on the weekends.

Once you have evaluated the place you volunteer, what responsibilities you have, and what roles you have assumed, discussing your activities with your manager could take place in several different ways. Of course your formal performance review or semi-annual discussions would be appropriate times. There is, however, a strategy that should be employed to make the greatest positive impact for your professional development.

Determining what your ultimate goal is in sharing the information with your boss is the first step. If the skills you are using in volunteering are not ones you can use in your current role, but would be valuable in other departments or positions within the organization, then an annual performance review may be the better time to bring up the topic. Annual reviews are typically the time to have a formalized two-way discussion about what you provide to the company and what the company is committing to provide you – beyond a paycheck. In later chapters we will go into greater detail about the performance review process and content and how to best approach this with your manager.

If your objective in speaking with your boss about your volunteering is to suggest ideas for how your team could get involved in a team building activity, then the discussion could be conducted at any point. Remember that your manager may or may not see value in having the team get involved, so set your expectations realistically so you are not disappointed. Having a trial discussion that is very top line about volunteering as a concept will give you a temperature check on his possible reaction.

For those of you who work in companies committed to community involvement, you have a unique scenario. On one hand, the company may already be doing volunteering as a group or at certain times of the year. If that is the situation, then you should evaluate what role you could have to support the existing programs. No one wants their employees to come in and think that their idea is going to replace a program that has benefited the employees and the community in the past.

This is a common occurrence that people overlook. Does your company do a toy drive or food drive during the holidays? What have you done to actively participate in that activity? How can you get involved to increase the participation from your department or team? Could you establish a role or function that improves the results of the team moving forward? Having external experience in volunteering puts you in a position to provide recommendations that could provide a new perspective or idea to expand the previous commitment or results from the team.

You may be surprised how many opportunities there are for you to help in existing projects or programs to support your company's involvement in the community. Talk to your peers and HR to see what activities the company is doing outside the workplace. It's possible that your manager or team is not currently informed or engaged in opportunities to work in the community. Thinking outside the box and researching internally outside your scope and department could help your team and management to have a plan and actions to support a companywide vision.

Employees who are in organizations not involved in community service at all are in a unique position. The first step is to do some investigation on why the company has not participated in the past. There may be a situation to be sensitive to in your approach of a discussion with your manager. Community service is a dynamic that has really blossomed since the late 90's. There are organizations that are not in a position to invest time into this volunteerism at this point. Understanding the type of company you work for is very important.

Your volunteering location may be an opportunity for the team to offer their skills to an underserved organization. This doesn't mean that everyone on the team needs to participate. Evaluate what your goal is. If you are positioning your experience outside of work as a value add to your work team, then you need to be well versed in the value the participants will have from being at the location and how that could translate into your company. A toy drive may not seem like a value added experience to some people, but there are plenty of organizations which use that type of activity to maximize their employees' abilities to provide value to the communities they serve.

Networking in volunteering is another valuable part of the experience to both you and your company. The bottom line is if you are investing a significant amount of time in volunteering and are using skills applicable to your current role or one that is in your career path, you'll benefit from informing management. Companies want to support employees in all of their goals to be better people at work and in their communities – volunteer experience is a significant part of this. Take time to evaluate what you do in your volunteering, have notes on how your responsibilities and roles are aligned with your current job function or the one you are trying to achieve in your career path, and establish the goals of a discussion with your boss of the experience.

If you are investing time to provide value to an external organization with skills that your job requires, your employer will value it too. Whether you live in a major metro or rural community, networking and commitment to the overall benefit of the people the organization serves is a primary focus. You are providing value and if your current employer doesn't identify that as important, you will find those skills valuable in your career at another time.

Take the time to dig deep in your current organization to find places that will value the time and effort you are devoting to that experience in your personal life. You may be surprised how your interests outside the workplace will support your professional development path. The department or team you are part of may not be actively involved in supporting volunteerism, but bringing it to their attention could position you as someone who takes a bigger picture view of how your team can bring value to the larger organization.

I know how to write the measured parts of my performance review **I think** ...

The next chapters are going to examine how to take an active role in your performance discussions. For some people these discussions are informal and spontaneous, and others it will be formal and scheduled at certain times dictated by the organization. Either way, as an employee of a large, medium or small company, it is your responsibility to own how you receive feedback and how you plan to respond with information about your performance. Individuals who do their job and then wait for the next time the boss is ready to nail them with negative input or pat them on the back with kudos are not taking control of their professional development in the workplace.

It really doesn't matter what industry you work in, there will be part of your job that is measured in some way. You may not think that you are being measured in some cases, because the company hasn't announced specific metrics for evaluation for that time period or year. The best way to determine what you may be measured on is to read your job description. Look for words like 'timely', 'meeting deadlines', 'achieving', and 'exceeding'. If there are parts of your job that have numerical values attached by their very nature – sales, growth, reduction in events, percentage improvement in profit or loss – these are the obvious things that will come up during performance conversations.

The next determination of what you may be measured on should be areas that your manager is measured on. There is a great possibility that if your boss is measured on 'on time performance' – you will be too. Those of you who aspire to fill your boss's shoes at some point in the future, it is a good idea to get a copy of his job description so you know what you may be signing up for. For employees who don't want the vertical path, but more of a horizontal one, understanding your manager's job will help you be a better employee. When he comes to you with a high sense of urgency about a certain project/ process/procedure you will not worry about 'where did that come from' and will be more focused on 'how can I support and assist him'. Having that perspective will carry you a long way in your immediate job and ultimately give you skills for the long term too.

Once you understand what you will be evaluated on that is going to be measured – not subjective items, those are addressed in the next chapter – you will need to do several things to make sure you are informed and ready to have performance discussions when your manager needs to. The most skilled employees at managing their own professional development have their fingers constantly on the pulse of where they stand with factors that are measured in their job performance. Whether it is the ability to be on time to work, deadlines on projects, sales objectives, reductions in turnover as a manager, or the skill to bring in new talent to the organization, the people who consistently earn pay increases and make more money in organizations year after year know how they are measured and where they stand at any point in time during the fiscal year.

Reports are the easiest way to see where you stand on the measure-ables. But what can you do when the reports are sent sporadically or not available to you at all? Anytime your manager works with you and shares their perspective on your ability to perform on the things that he is measured on, ask for copies of that information. He should be able to give you a broad viewpoint on where you fall within all of his direct reports in that area.

What is the motivation for your manager to keep you informed on where you stand on the measureables? First off, if you don't know where you stand, you can't establish where you need to go. Second, you can't be held accountable for things if you cannot establish an action plan that will allow you to improve. Even if your manager can't give you the actual reports, he should be able to let you know where you can improve your performance or in what areas you can get more training, experience, or skills to have a more positive result.

So how should you respond if your boss wants you to write your own performance review? First of all, be thankful you get a chance to represent yourself. Secondly, take the time to double check what information you have, and what information you need to get to be accurate in your input. The last thing you want to have happen is that your boss reviews your input and finds errors in the calculations or measurements. Even if the results are not painting a rosy picture of your performance in every area, you will need to include it if it is a metric in your review.

The benefit of being able to write the measured part yourself is that you can also include information that explains the results. Don't confuse this with being able to 'justify' or 'excuse' the results. Explanation means providing facts and information that is data based and non-emotional. Even if there isn't a section on a form to add comments, you could add an asterisk at the end of a numerical value and then make a notation at the end of the page or the end of the performance review document. If you don't have a formal process for review and the discussion with your manager is more laid back, you should still be prepared with the measurable results and why you achieved them. The most highly valued employees will be able to separate the emotions from the actions and accurately explain the how, when, where, and why of each measurable result.

If you aren't able to write the initial version of your performance in measurable areas, how can you make sure the information is an accurate representation of what you have accomplished on the tangible factors that determine your value to the company? Not being able to take total control of the process and output doesn't mean that you won't have a say in the final document that goes into your personnel file. Identify what the process is – does your manager put together the fact based information of your reports and then ask you for the 'how did you do it' part? Is it a process that dictates that the report is the bottom line?

Whatever the process is, as a valuable part of the organization, you should know the way the process works and at what point you are able to give input or information. There is a reality to the process that each employee needs to acknowledge however. In the measurables, some parts will be undisputable, non-negotiable, and indefensible. Maybe you were late to work 5% of the year – this isn't up for discussion. It is a fact that can be documented by time cards and your own ability to use a punch clock effectively. In these instances, you are not going to have an opportunity to provide the myriad of reasons you did not meet the expectation of your role to be on time.

Part of the privilege to write or provide input on the measurable parts of your performance review involves the responsibility to own the good, bad, and ugly of the year's outcomes and data driven results. If you are not prepared to accept all of the process, you can't accurately document and celebrate your successes and you can't identify and learn from your developmental opportunities. The highest performing employees are willing to accept it all and move on to the subjective parts of the performance discussions with business acumen and understanding.

I understand how to write the subjective parts of my performance review I think ...

Depending on your industry and the size of the organization you work in, you may find that your performance review (or informal discussion) is primarily subjective. This is the 80's version of 'good ole boys' performance discussions – "you're doing a great job, just keep it up", "Can't think of anything you could do better", "Stay focused on sales and you'll be a winner"... The bottom line of a completely subjective performance review is that the employee is going to be the one who needs to own the process and outcomes.

The good news is that there are very few companies that conduct performance discussions exclusively around subjective measures now. Part of that is due to labor lawsuits and people acknowledging that there should be a measuring stick to help managers define what good looks like. Really, subjective measures come down to just that – what do 'good', 'great', and 'excellent' look like. Most companies have a monitor for those measurements in subjective levels – the HR department. Even though 'subjective' implies that the manager can have their own opinion, there needs to be a justification for the content.

It may be a reasonable expectation in your field or industry that each employee provides input and content for the subjective parts of their performance reviews. For example, people in outside sales oftentimes work in offices far away from their direct supervisors and peers. In these circumstances, it would be hard for someone on the team to comment about consistent ways you showed leadership, customer service, or problem-solving skills.

On the other hand, i you work in an ofice setting where you see your direct supervisor and your peers on a daily basis, the subjective content of your performance could include information from all of the people who interact with you. Remember the reference in previous chapters to the importance of having your peers and manager understand your value in contributing to the overall performance of the team or growth of current and new team members? This becomes very important in this type of subjective performance measurement.

Subjective could imply to the employee that there is an opinion or feeling offered in providing the information or output. When it comes to performance of your job, you do not want to get into a 'he said – she said' fight with your peers or your manager. The best deense is a strong œnse – understanding what parts o your job and results are subject to this type of evaluation will help you be prepared and informed.

Be aware that the subjective parts of your performance review will also be the ones where your manager could be emotional or reactive to your attitude and morale in the workplace. Factors such as your ability to manage change (versus complain) or ability to ask questions (versus stating obstacles) will be important in these sections of your performance discussions. There are few employees that care about their jobs and companies that don't have emotional moments throughout the year. It's important to know when those moments occurred and then identify why, when and how you handled the situation that time and what you did to learn from the experience to further your professional development to benefit the team.

So, what do you do when your boss makes comments in the subjective part of your review that surprised you in a positive way? THANK THEM. That may seem obvious, but there are some employees that feel they don't need to appreciate their manager for positive feedback – they are the ones that will not have a long term career path. It doesn't matter whether you are an employee, manager, or owner, you want to have someone appreciate your acknowledgement of their positive performance.

What i the comments are not so positive? The first step is to take a breath… Don't get emotional – period. This is about your performance in your job. At the end of the day, you want to stay employed in this role for now, and trying to do a better job. You can go home and think that your manager is insane, needs a new reporting system to accurately evaluate your abilities, or should stop looking at the one report that makes him judge the rest of your performance in a subjectively negative way.

Here is your opportunity for truly professional development. Read the section or sections of your review that are less positive than you would have preferred. Break the information up like you would i you had a grocery list – are there only produce items to purchase (communication issues to work on), could you purchase better quality meat products (opportunities for leadership that you missed or didn't execute well). The point is not to get wrapped up in the emotion of 'I don't do X well', and instead examine why your manager noted the different areas.

Remember that the subjective areas of your performance discussions could lead to the most emotional parts of conversations with your manager. Take the emotion out of it on your side as much as possible. Saying 'I can see how that situation seemed like X' or 'Could you help me to understand how I could have Y' will allow your manage an opportunity to explain their perception without feeling like you are being confrontational.

The subjective parts of performance discussions are the most un-comfortable for managers. It really doesn't matter whether you are telling a high performing employee how great they are, or trying to coach someone who needs to focus and get it together in order to stay in their current job, it's a weird position. Managers who are giving someone an 'way to go' for an amazing job, have to position that in the context that the employee still has room to grow. For those that really need to improve their results to stay on the team, the boss needs to provide direction on how they can do that without demotivating them and sending them into 'job search mode'.

Ultimately, the subjective parts of a review will determine the ways your manager will try and view you throughout the next quarter, half, or year. Because these are the 'soft skills' in most cases, there will be multiple opportunities for you to exhibit your abilities to use and develop them. Your job function and exposure to internal and external constituents will provide situations for you to show how you can, and have, developed abilities in those areas.

Understanding what those skills and abilities are is important, but understanding how your boss values and ranks those in importance to your overall performance is crucial. Sure, it's great for a salesperson to know how to communicate effectively. Depending on the type of product or service they provide, communication could be the cornerstone of their ability to achieve measurables in closing the sale. Establishing what your manager's position is on the core behaviors needed to be productive in your role is very important. Every person employed on the planet needs to be able to speak to someone at some point in their job. That doesn't mean that everyone needs the same level of communication abilities to do every job.

This book is aimed at empowering you to take responsibility for your job and roles throughout your career. Part of that ownership is learning, understanding, and growing professionally from discussions with your manager. The next chapter examines how your current performance discussions can pave the way for your next project, internal opportunity, lateral move, vertical position, or cross-industry strategy.

I communicate my expectations for profes-

sional development to my boss I think ...

Every performance discussion with your boss should include your ideas about what your short and long term professional goals are. You don't have to plan to move into your boss' job in the next year to make this a worthwhile discussion. Since your performance review should cover things you do well, in addition to things you could do better, it makes sense that you establish a plan for how to become better skilled and more effective in your current role.

Think about this part of your conversation in sections – what can you do to be better in your current job, what can you do to figure out what future positions you may want within the company, how can you get the training and skills you need to move into the next career opportunity, and ultimately what is your goal to potentially move into positions in the long term.

The most valued employees don't sit back and become complacent once they master the basic responsibilities of their role. In previous chapters we discussed how you can add value to an organization by learning new skills or improving ones that you need to make the team better. Asking your boss what you can do to be better in your current job allows you to have a candid discussion about your strengths and weaknesses.

Even the most talented people in one area will have opportunities to improve in others. Consider the abilities of Steve Jobs during his time at Apple. His desire to constantly look for the newest, most progressive, highest functioning hardware led to the iPod, iPad, and countless other technological wonders that are currently in development. It was well known that for all of his strategic brilliance, Steve also had challenges verbally communicating with peers and subordinates. He even lost it and got overly emotional in meetings with his team.

Did this form of communication make him less effective? Possibly. It's a safe bet that more than once during his interactions with his superiors or peers he received feedback about increasing his tolerance for others and as well as his patience during stressful meetings. He may have even been asked to take a class or learn techniques to calm down before unloading his feelings on people in the workplace.

When you are preparing for your performance discussions, you should be willing to take a step back and honestly evaluate how you could improve your skills and value to the company.

Previously we addressed how to use mentoring or training to expand your value to the team. This may also be a way for you to establish what positions within the company may fit your career aspirations. Perhaps you will discover by helping others that you want to move into a management role. Maybe assisting others to be better in an area that you excel in will motivate you to pursue an opportunity in formal training positions. Working with new hires may generate a desire to consider a human resources role.

Another way to determine options for your internal career path is to request opportunities to shadow people on other teams or in departments that your team interacts with. Getting the perspective of someone in a totally different function within the organization could open your eyes to ways your strengths could be utilized in a completely different capacity than your current role allows you to use them. You may also provide those people in the company with a perspective that will result in improved cross-functional performance.

Your performance review discussion of continuing your professional development doesn't need to be completely planned out in advance by you, but having a few ideas of where you want to potentially grow will help you have a productive conversation that can lead to creation of an action plan. Once you have a list of options, take the time to identify the skills or training you will need to move into those types of positions.

Showing up to the meeting with your manager and announcing 'I want to be a manager' is not going to be as productive as 'I believe my skills in coaching people informally could be used effectively in a management role. I would like to talk about ways I can continue to support our team in mentoring and also expand my exposure to other departments by shadowing Tom. I have found a management communications workshop through our training team that can also help me build the skills to be an effective manager.'

The next important step is to ask your boss to support you in each of these activities. Obviously, you won't be able to shadow people in other departments without your manager making some calls and asking for collaboration with those teams. He will also need to establish that each of these steps is important in your overall development plan. Requesting that you document each of these ideas will accomplish two important things. First, you have a formal acceptance and agreement of the next steps that you and your boss will take to execute the plan. Second, you will start the clock on accomplishing the steps.

The final step is to communicate formally what your longer term goals are for internal development within the organization. Why is this a significant step? Management personnel could change, your department could merge, the company could be acquired –

bottom line is that you won't be able to control every business dynamic that could support or derail your development plan.

Remember in the movie Pretty Woman how Julia Roberts' roommate at the end of the movie is talking with a prospective new roommate and says 'Do you have plan? Cause you need to have a plan.' This statement is vital to consistency in your ability to progress, independent of the uncontrollable factors of business. Even if you leave your current employer you could take your overall development plan and execute it somewhere else. Every company has some sort of training process or department. Managers will always want to have people continue to build their professional skills, especially if that will help the team be better and add more value to the organization.

I effectively prepare for my performance discussions with my boss I think ...

Throughout the year you have planned and executed the various ways recommended in the previous chapters to show your manager how valuable you can be to the company. Now it's time for your performance discussion. Can't you just show up and know that your boss has taken note of all your work appropriately and will now recognize you for it? No, you can't. The reality is that your manager probably has more than just you to think about during each workday. Don't assume he has kept detailed notes of all that you've done in your basic job function or the above and beyond work, because he likely has not.

Even if your manager only has you reporting to him, he will need to be keeping track of his own performance to discuss with his boss. The biggest mistake people make in managing their career and professional development is that they don't take control of it. It is your job to take the notes throughout the year, keep copies of the 'way to go' emails, and document the ways you succeeded and supported the team.

So, what are the things to be sure to have for the performance discussion? First take a look at the notes you have from your last performance discussion with your boss. Evaluate your performance against the measurable objectives you set, the training and skills you wanted to gain, and the ways you planned to further your experience to increase your value to the company. Write down how you believe you should be rated in these areas.

Get organized with visuals to backup your evaluation in each area. This might include sales reports, emails from internal or external customers you interacted with, projects you led or collaborated with people on, and results from programs or projects you participated in. Depending on your role within the organization, you may be able to bring a few key things that correlate directly to visually showing your boss what you have done to accomplish your job and go beyond the basics in that timeframe.

Be careful not to overwhelm your manager with the encyclopedia of how awesome you were in the past quarter or year. Prepare enough to focus on the key skills that are predefined from your previous discussion or have been added in less formal conversations. For example, if you requested to mentor new employees in a certain area, sharing a schedule of whom you worked with along with a couple of emails from them thanking you for your time and support would be appropriate. Bringing in the company procedure manual and walking your boss page by page through every conversation you had with the new hires would be excessive.

Another important part of the preparation is to make an organized copy of these materials to leave with your manager. Even though he may be giving you his full attention during the discussion, the odds are that he will have to rewrite or add to your written appraisal based on information you talk about and show him. Providing him the details in hard copy will make his job easier in representing the true value you added to the company. Remember that making your boss' job easier will also make your work life more enjoyable.

For those of you in jobs that are management based or visual in nature, you may want to prepare a portfolio that may have additional information to show your boss. Managers may use performance reports from their employees, graphic artists may include design projects, and architects may share blueprints or drafts. Think about what other information could add value to the conversation in backing up your position on your performance. You may not need to make copies of all of these materials, but having them to represent your skills and experience could be the icing on the cake to get you the appraisal you want.

Your preparation also includes the research and notes on how you want to develop your skills to support your career development. This should be short and sweet. Have options to discuss with your manager, but don't bring in the whole training catalog to talk about in detail.

I'm confident enough to ask my boss for a pay increase I think ...

You've prepared for the performance discussion with what you have done, what you are going to do, and what you want to do in the short and long term to support the organization with your skills. The time has come to plan how and when you are going to go for it. In many companies, there is a formal timing and process to ensure that all employees have a chance to talk with their managers about what they did, what they need to do, and how they need to do it.

If your company has a formal performance review in the middle and end of the year, you will have to go through each of the steps in preparation for both discussions. Mid-year reviews may be less formal, but remember that there will be documentation of how you are doing at that point against measurable objectives. A review in the middle of the year is also an opportunity to discuss modifying objectives or adding new ones based on business changes, market dynamics, or personnel shifts.

A mid-year review isn't typically going to be the time to ask your boss for a pay increase. Companies that have both a midyear and formal annual review will be planning to provide increases annually based on iscal projections and plans. This doesn't mean you shouldn't be laying the groundwork for the year-end discussion at the midyear review. Establishing your value to the company mid-year will allow you to reinforce it at the year-end discussion.

In a formal annual performance review, there are some important things to know about how the conversation will typically go. Your manager will want to go through what he's prepared in his evaluation of your performance. This could include measurables on certain areas and subjective evaluation of other objectives. Having prepared information to back up your evaluation of these sections, you should be ready to add visuals and comments that are fact-based to each area. Letting your manager take the lead will be the most productive way to know what he has already recognized as your skills in each area. This process also lets him acknowledge the information you can add to what he has already prepared.

In an informal performance review, your manager may let you take the lead on the conversation. This type of discussion is where your preparation from the previous chapter is crucial. Being organized with information from your previous discussions and how you have performed against the various objectives and goals will keep you and your manager focused on the important ways you have added value to the team.

Whether you are in a formal or informal review discussion, asking your boss for a pay increase requires an understanding of different factors in your company. Do your homework. Know what the pay range is for your job function and where you stand on that range. Heading into a performance review asking for a 20% pay increase when you are at the top of your pay range is probably not realistic.

Understand how you could get the increase you want through different options. What if they changed your title based on your experience, skills, and performance throughout the year? Maybe the pay range for a Junior Territory Representative has a pay scale of $30K - $45K per year and the pay range for a Senior Territory Representative has a pay scale of $46K – 60K. Knowing the difference in the job descriptions and being able to express how your skills could fit the Senior Rep position will allow you to have a meaningful talk with your boss. He may not realize that changing your title and adding some responsibili-ties to your job – that you can handle and have showed you have the skills for – can allow him leeway in giving you a pay increase.

If changing your level, title, or job responsibilities can't allow flexibility for the pay increase you are requesting, consider other ways people have secured incremental pay in the past. Maybe someone on your team attended training or classes that gave them skills recognized by your company at a different level. Perhaps someone in another department became the official trainer in an area and was given an increase for taking on that responsibility. You will increase your chances of securing the incremental pay by providing options to your manager that have been done in the company previously – precedence always helps your boss justify the 'why' to his superiors.

Another factor that influences your pay increase discussion is timing. Yes, you will need to get a little charged up to be prepared to ask for a pay increase. This doesn't mean you can walk into the room, dump all of your documentation on how great an employee you are on the desk and demand more money. Actions like this could get you a quick trip to the unemployment line. You want your boss to consider the pay increase as a logical step based on what you have done and what you can do for the company. Acting entitled or self-absorbed will only alienate your manager and create an environment where he feels like he needs to push back and explain why you don't deserve a raise.

Think about discussions you have had with your parents, a significant other, or a close friend in the past. Did you talk to them about how you needed something from them when they are totally stressed out or focused on other personal issues? If you did, you probably didn't get what you asked for. This same concept holds true for asking your manager for support in getting a pay increase. If it's a formal discussion, you may not be able to choose the

I think

timing, but you need to be sensitive to the other things going on that are potential distraction and pressure factors for your manager. In an informal discussion, postpone it if you know that you are going to be fighting an uphill battle to get to a 'yes, I will support that'.

Your approach of the topic is going to play a large role in what your chances are to have your boss even consider giving you a pay increase, let alone fighting for you if he needs to. Focus on the word 'asking'. You should provide documentation, fact-based support, and passion for how your skills are important to your job function and the team, but your tone should show confidence and appreciation. If you have done your preparation to share information with your boss so he can document to others how you have supported the company, then he will be motivated to support your request.

The detail in what you ask for will depend on your role and industry. In certain fields, it may be acceptable to say 'based on my performance over the past year, is it reasonable for me to request a 3% increase in pay?' In others, you may want to toss the ball into your manager's side of the court to initiate a discussion by saying 'I believe my skills and performance over the past year show my commitment to our team. What level of pay increase would be available based on my performance?'

Your manager may not have had anyone show up to a performance discussion this prepared before. He may be a little taken aback by you actually knowing what is realistic to ask for and then asking for it. That is ok. As long as you aren't approaching the topic like a bull in a china shop you can help him with data and documents to achieve your objective. Being prepared with information, stating your value without emotion, and giving your boss fact-based ammunition to get you a pay increase will lead to a successful discussion for both of you.

I'm ready for my review I think ...

_____

Here's a final checklist to help you make sure you have a professional discussion with your manager that will establish what you have accomplished, where you want to improve, and what your short and long term development goals are. Be sure you:

- Understand how co-workers may describe your performance if management asks

- Review all midyear (or previous performance discussion) plans and know your results against each of the areas

- Prepare documentation on the ways you have assisted co-workers which resulted in making the company better

- Identify ways to be an informal or formal leader in your department, or in support of other departments, since the last performance discussion and moving forward

- Can describe how being an expert in certain skills or job functions provide value to the team

- Know how you have used your skills to support the newer members, as a tenured member of the team

- Have information about the ways you assisted your manager in their job and supported their objectives

- Are prepared to explain how skills used outside the workplace in volunteering, and/or being a leader in a volunteer organization translated into your job

- Identify ways to expand your development and career path through training and development of additional skills

- Review the measured parts of your performance and have detailed information in support of what rating or feedback you expect from your manager

- Evaluate the subjective sections of your performance and can communicate the results you achieved

- Create a rationale and information to establish action plans for professional development in order to move into the next role or expand your professional growth in your existing position

- Understand that asking for a pay increase is a process with a balance of information of what you have done to perform effectively, how you have added value outside your job description, and what you are planning to do to add value

One last note:

Getting a pay increase may seem like a reasonable annual activity for some people and like a challenge for others. Using this book to accurately evaluate how you have planned and executed throughout a year to show your value to an employers will allow you to provide evidence of the why, when, and where you have earned the right to ask for the incremental compensation.

Extra Resources:

---

www.bestresumebuilder.com

- If you want to use a program which will walk you through, step by step in less than 45 minutes, the input which creates a great resume - check out this resource. Created specifically to be detailed on input to create a dynamic resume, it's specific and easy to use.

Salary Calculators

- There are several online salary calculators that can give you an estimation of what people in your type of position are being paid in your geography.

Index

Also available in the *(I think)* ™ *Career Skills Series:*

Acknowledgements

For my family and friends who contributed their input and support to this book.

About the Author

Stacie Garlieb is the President of Successful Impressions LLC which assists collegiates and working professionals with career search processes and skills. She has been featured several times on NBC television and radio during morning and evening news with interview tips. Stacie is a well-known national speaker who has presented on various career skills topics at events such as 'Build Your Career Event' (Career Builder/University of Phoenix), Arizona Women's Expo. American Marketing Association International Conferences, Jobs for AZ Graduates Career Development Conferences, and Reinvent Your Future. Her career search tips and interview skills advice have been published in collegiate, national sorority, and alumni publications. Through group presentations and one-on-one coaching on all career search related topics, she has worked with public and private college students nationally since 1991. In collaboration with businesses in various fields, she actively develops internship programs and recruits at public and private universities as well as career fairs.

If you would like to know more about Stacie Garlieb's company or her seminars please visit her website at www.successfulimpressions.net

www.ingramcontent.com/pod-product-compliance
Lightning Source LLC
Chambersburg PA
CBHW051242170526
45165CB00004B/1541